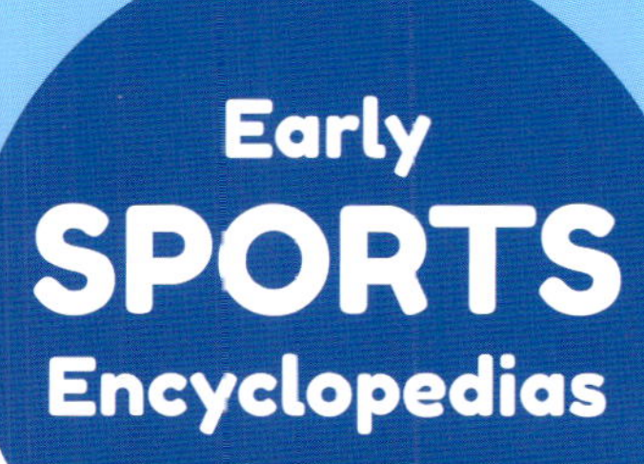

GYMNASTICS

by Karen Price

An Imprint of Abdo Reference
abdobooks.com

abdobooks.com

Published by Abdo Reference, a division of ABDO, PO Box 398166, Minneapolis, Minnesota 55439. Copyright © 2024 by Abdo Consulting Group, Inc. International copyrights reserved in all countries. No part of this book may be reproduced in any form without written permission from the publisher. Early Encyclopedias™ is a trademark and logo of Abdo Reference.

Printed in China
052023
092023

THIS BOOK CONTAINS
RECYCLED MATERIALS

Editor: Priscilla An
Series Designers: Candice Keimig, Joshua Olson

Library of Congress Control Number: 2022949128

Publisher's Cataloging-in-Publication Data

Names: Price, Karen, author.
Title: Gymnastics / by Karen Price
Description: Minneapolis, Minnesota: Abdo Reference, 2024 | Series: Early sports encyclopedias | Includes online resources and index.
Identifiers: ISBN 9781098291297 (lib. bdg.) | ISBN 9781098277475 (ebook)
Subjects: LCSH: Gymnastics--Juvenile literature. | Gymnasts--Juvenile literature. | Team sports--Juvenile literature. | Sports--History--Juvenile literature. | Encyclopedias and dictionaries--Juvenile literature.
Classification: DDC 796.03--dc23

CONTENTS

Gymnastics is an exciting sport. People can learn the basic moves from a young age. Gymnasts usually perform their moves on special equipment, such as rings and the balance beam. Each piece of equipment is called an apparatus.

In artistic gymnastics, boys, girls, men, and women have different events. Some are the same. Women compete in vault, uneven bars, balance beam, and floor exercise. Men compete in floor exercise, pommel horse, still rings, vault, parallel bars, and horizontal bar.

A gymnastics competition is called a meet. Gymnastics meets often include multiple competitions. One is the all-around competition.

An Olympic gymnasium needs to be big enough to fit the various gymnastics apparatuses.

In the all-around, each gymnast competes on every apparatus. The final score combines all the results. There are also competitions for each apparatus. Finally, there is a team competition.

There are many skills required of a gymnast. As gymnasts get better and learn more skills, they move up levels. The highest level is elite.

Gymnasts become more flexible as they learn more skills.

FUN FACT!

In 1996, Dominique Dawes was the first Black woman to win an individual medal in Olympic gymnastics with the bronze in the floor exercise. She is one of only three American women to have competed in three Olympics.

Those are the gymnasts who compete at international competitions including the Olympics and World Championships.

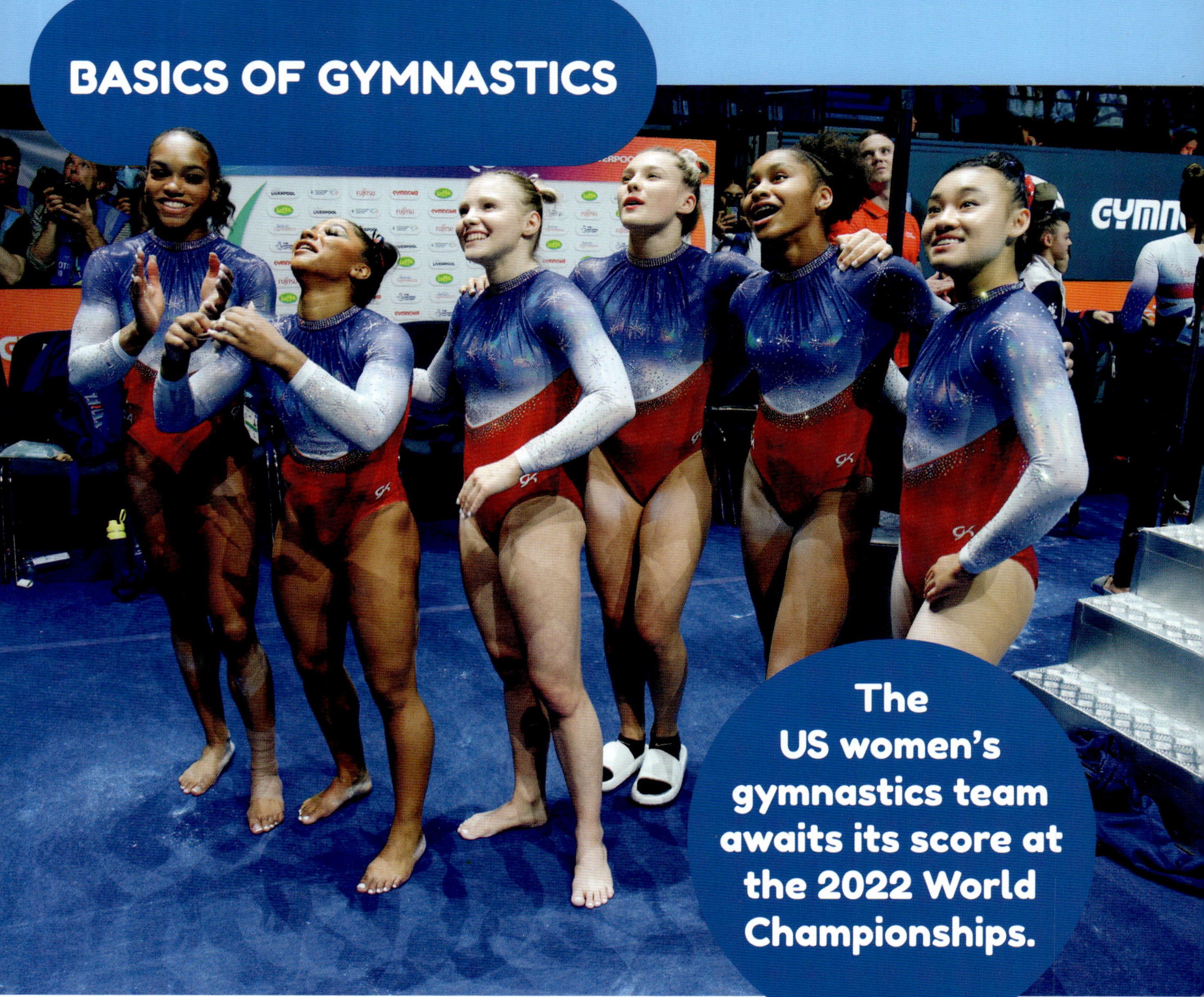

The US women's gymnastics team awaits its score at the 2022 World Championships.

Scoring

Scoring gymnastics has changed over the years. The "perfect 10" used to be the best score a gymnast could get. It still is at some levels of the sport. Elite gymnastics now uses an "open-ended" system.

Each routine receives two scores. One is based on difficulty. A group of judges adds points based on requirements and how hard the skills are. The other score is based on execution. The highest possible execution score is 10. A second group of judges takes away points for mistakes. For a final score, the difficulty value and execution score are combined. Scores at international competitions will often be between 13 and 16 points.

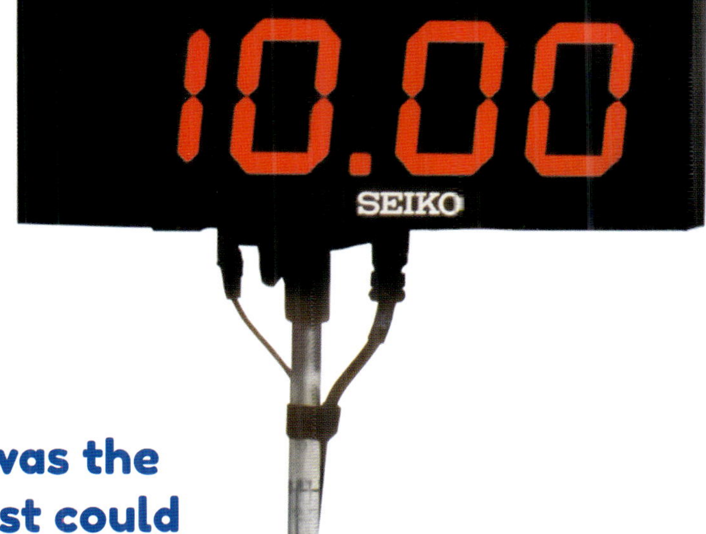

Before 2006, a 10 was the best score a gymnast could receive for a routine.

Flexibility is necessary when performing gymnastics skills.

Artistry

Gymnastics combines strength, power, grace, and courage. When people start taking gymnastics lessons, they will learn to perform skills that may seem impossible. Gymnasts can do things no one else can do!

Artistry is a big part of gymnastics. Judges look at it during a routine. Gymnasts are expected to show their style and originality. They express themselves

FUN FACT!

Gymnasts often put chalk on their hands. It's made of magnesium carbonate and stops their hands from getting sweaty. That gives them a better grip on the bars.

during their routines. The most popular type of gymnastics is called artistic gymnastics. Olympic gold medalists Simone Biles and Suni Lee do artistic gymnastics.

Floor Exercise

Both men and women compete in floor exercise. They use a 40-foot by 40-foot (12.2 m by 12.2 m) square mat. Springs make it bouncy. Women perform their routines to music. Men do not. Women's routines are also longer.

Tumbling passes are a big part of a floor routine. Gymnasts link different skills together to create them. Some of these basic skills include forward rolls, backward rolls, and cartwheels. More advanced skills include walkovers, handsprings, and flips. Gymnasts need to be careful. A gymnast who goes out of bounds will lose points. Gymnasts always want to stick their landings.

A women's floor routine needs more than just tumbling. Gymnasts have to show artistry.

Unlike the men's floor exercise routine, women compete with music.

Gymnasts perform dance moves such as leaps and turns in between tumbling passes. These demonstrate grace and creativity. Men's routines are focused on strength and power. They do more tumbling in their routines than women do.

Floor Exercise Moves

Balance Beam

To be good on the balance beam, gymnasts need balance. The beam is only 4 inches (10 cm) wide. That's slightly wider than a smartphone. If they don't have good balance, gymnasts will quickly fall off.

Gymnasts competed on the balance beam at the Olympics for the first time in 1952. The first American woman to win gold on the balance beam was Shannon Miller in 1996.

The balance beam is often called the beam. Only women compete on the beam. New gymnasts don't start there. They learn on the floor and practice on a beam that's closer to the ground. That helps build confidence. Confidence is important on every apparatus.

Gymnasts keep their balance by making sure their arms and legs are in the right places.

Gymnasts start a beam routine with a mount. They can mount from the side or the end of the beam. Beam routines include leaps and turns. Advanced gymnasts will combine difficult tumbling moves including handsprings and saltos.

Join a Club

Many cities have gymnastics clubs. They will often let new students watch classes before joining. Some clubs are more competitive than others. It's important to meet the instructors and ask questions. This will help a gymnast find the right fit.

If a gymnast falls off, she is allowed to get back on. She'll lose points for the fall. Points can be taken off for grabbing the beam or for bobbling. When a gymnast loses her balance and almost falls but recovers in time, it's called a bobble. At the end of the routine, gymnasts perform a dismount and land back on the ground.

It can
take a lot
of practice
before a gymnast
is confident on
the balance
beam.

Vault

The vault is the quickest of all the gymnastics events. It lasts only a few seconds from start to finish. Both men and women compete in the vault.

Gymnasts start by running as fast as they can toward a springboard. They jump on the springboard, then hit the vaulting table with their hands. That launches the gymnast into the air. Some of the hardest vaults are called Yurchenkos. Gymnasts do a roundoff before they reach the springboard and a back handspring onto the table. It's important to stick the landing!

When a gymnast's hands push off the vault table, it's called a block.

A powerful
run sets up
a vault.

In 2021, Simone Biles did a vault so difficult that no other woman had ever tried it in a competition. It's called a Yurchenko double pike.

Oksana Chusovitina is a vault specialist from Uzbekistan. She became the oldest Olympic gymnast ever when she competed in the Olympics in Tokyo, Japan, in 2021. She was 46 years old. It was her eighth time at the Olympics.

In 2021, Marian Drăgulescu became the oldest man to compete at the Olympics since 1960. He is from Romania and was 40 years old at the Tokyo Olympics. He has a vault named after him. The Drăgulescu is a handspring double front somersault vault with a half twist.

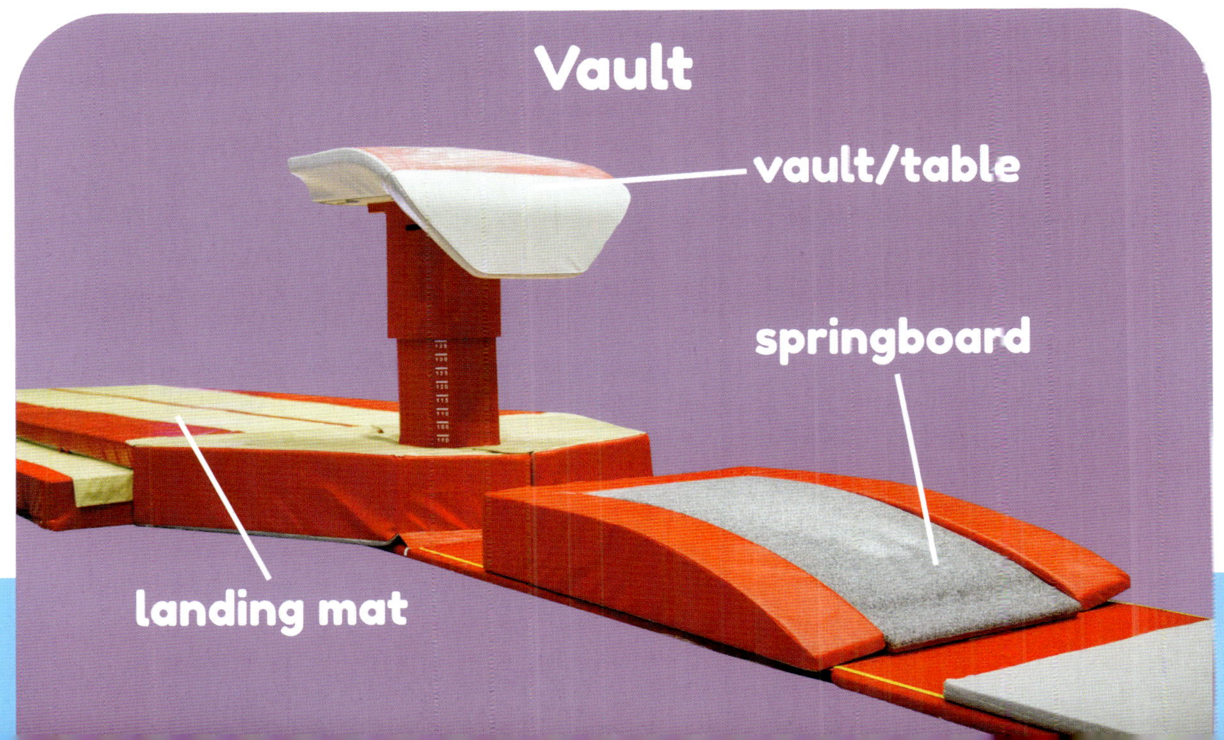

Uneven Bars

Uneven bars are another apparatus that only women use. The apparatus includes two bars. One bar is higher than the other bar. They are up to 6 feet (1.8 m) apart. Gymnasts move back and forth between the two during their routines.

Gymnasts can grip the bar in different ways. They can circle around the bars, going both forward and backward. Sometimes gymnasts do

handstands on a bar. They can also swing from bar to bar. This move is called a transition. Sometimes gymnasts fully let go of the bar.

Other times, gymnasts perform a release move. This is when they do a move in the air. Then they catch the bar again.

Suni Lee was the all-around champion at the Tokyo Olympics. She is also one of the best gymnasts in the world on the uneven bars. No one was doing a routine as hard as hers before the Tokyo Games.

Lee did four of the hardest moves in the sport. She did them all in a row. She had to be strong and exact. She could have lost

China's Wei Xiaoyuan does her routine at the 2022 World Championships.

her grip with even a small mistake. One move
was called a Nabieva. Lee started on the highest
bar. She did a handstand and then swung down.
Her legs were straight and touched the bar. She
swung back up and let go. She caught the bar
and went right to the next move.

Parallel Bars

Parallel means side by side.
This event uses two bars that are
the same height. Many gymnasts just call them
P bars. The bars are 6.5 feet (2 m) off the ground.
Only men compete in parallel bars.

Gymnasts sometimes put honey and chalk on their hands in order to improve their grip on the parallel bars.

A gymnast needs to have a strong upper body for parallel bars. One of the first things he will learn to do is hold himself above the bars with straight arms. Later, he will learn how to swing his body back and forth. Once the gymnast is skilled enough, he will be able to do a handstand.

Olympic routines include swinging moves and flight moves. That means a gymnast lets go of both bars and does a skill. Then he catches himself. Routines also include holds. Gymnasts will swing between and under the bars. They'll also swing above them. These routines require great endurance.

Trampoline and Tumbling

Another form of gymnastics is called trampoline and tumbling. There are four events. They are trampoline, power tumbling, synchronized trampoline, and double mini trampoline. Both men and women compete in all four events.

A routine might start with the gymnast swinging below the bars. Then he might hold himself up. His arms will be straight. His legs will be straight ahead. His body makes the shape of an *L*. His arms stay still as he pulls his legs between the bars and then up into a handstand. He gets ready to dismount with a flip to the ground.

Still Rings

It may look fun to swing back and forth on the rings. But in gymnastics, swinging too much will cost gymnasts points. To get a high score, it's important to keep the rings very still. It isn't easy to do.

The rings hang about 8 feet (2.4 m) off the ground.

Only men compete on rings. This apparatus requires very strong arm, shoulder, chest, and back muscles. A routine will have several different moves. The gymnast should rotate forward and backward. Handstands and other moves show strength, balance, and control.

One very hard move is called an iron cross. The gymnast makes a *T* with his body. He holds himself up with his arms straight out at his sides. He'll lose points if his body is too high or too low. Another very hard move is called a planche. The gymnast holds himself above the rings. He faces down. His whole body is parallel to the floor. Strength moves are also timed. Gymnasts must hold each one for two seconds. The routine ends with a dismount.

iron cross

planche

35

Pommel Horse

The pommel horse looks like a long, skinny table. The table is the "horse." The pommels are the two curved handles that are attached to the top of the table. This apparatus requires great strength. Balance and timing are also important. It takes a lot of practice to master.

Acrobatic Gymnastics

Another type of gymnastics is called acrobatic gymnastics. It's done in pairs or in groups. The athletes work together to balance and form shapes with their bodies. Acrobatic gymnastics combines dance, tumbling, and acrobatic moves.

Stephen Nedoroscik competes in the 2022 World Championships in Liverpool, England.

Only men compete on the pammel horse.
SPIETH
SPIETH

In this event, the gymnast uses his arms to hold his body up the entire time. Sometimes he holds onto both pommels. Sometimes he uses only one. Otherwise he can place his hands right on the table. The gymnast may move from

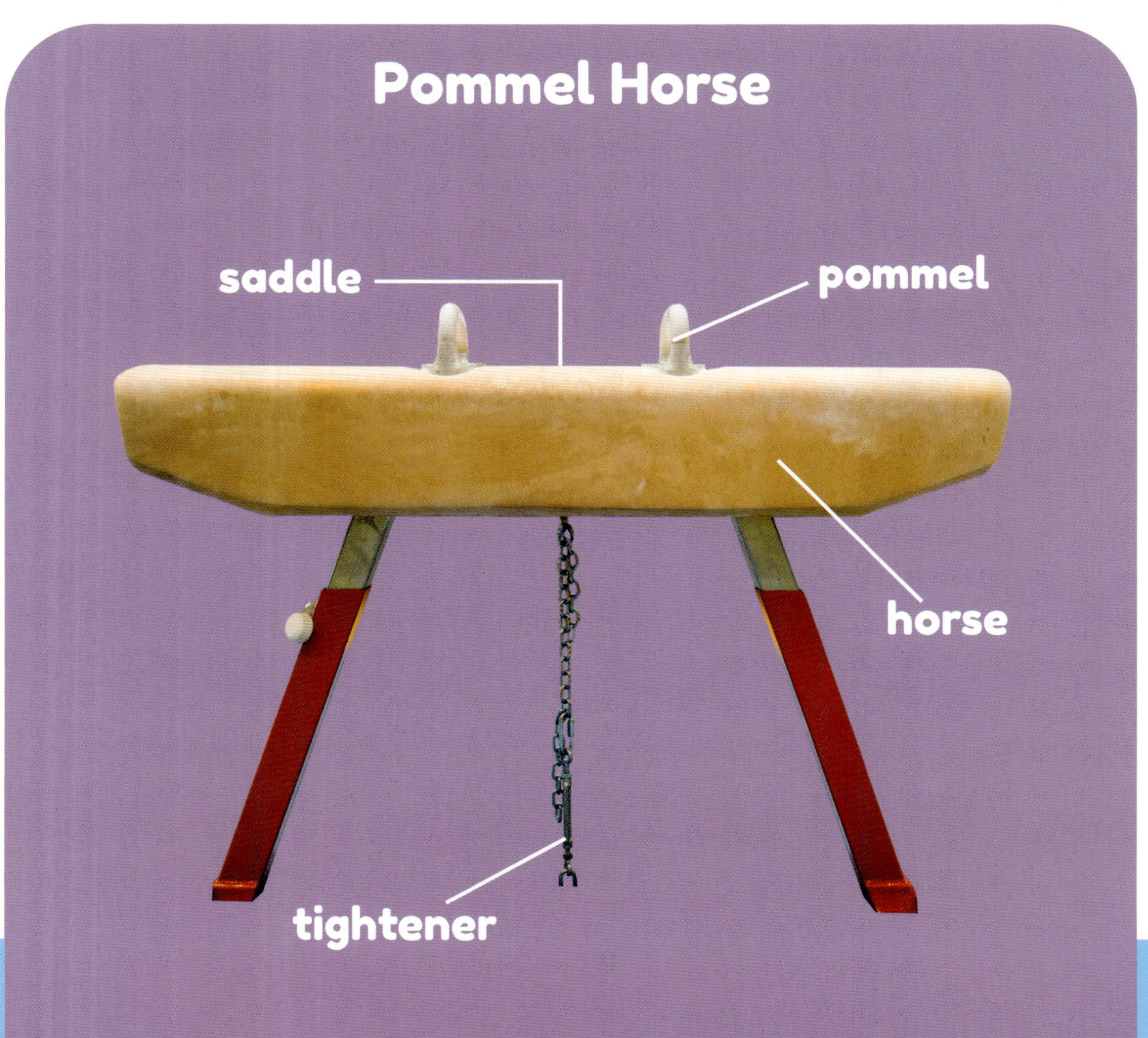

one end of the horse to the other. One move is called a double leg circle. The gymnast keeps his legs straight and together and swings them around in circles. There are also flares. In a flare, the gymnast's legs are wide apart. Gymnasts also swing their legs back and forth on either side of the horse. Those are called scissors.

Only a gymnast's hands can touch the horse. Hitting the horse with a leg might slow the gymnast's rhythm or knock him off-balance. He can restart if he stops, but he will lose points. Stephen Nedoroscik made history for the United States when he became the country's first world champion on the pommel horse in 2021.

Horizontal Bar

Women compete on uneven bars. However, men compete on just one bar. It's called the horizontal bar, or the high bar. The bar is more than 9 feet (2.7 m) off the ground.

A coach will lift the gymnast up to reach the bar and start the routine. The gymnast swings around the bar. His arms and legs stay perfectly straight. This move is called a giant swing.

Release moves are when the gymnast lets go of the bar. The gymnast might do somersaults through the air. Then he would catch the bar with his hands and swing.

Another move is called a Stalder.

FUN FACT!

In 2022, Brody Malone became the first US man to win gold on the horizontal bar at the World Championships in 43 years. The last American gymnast to win a world title on horizontal bar was Kurt Thomas in 1979.

Horizontal
bar routines
are usually 15
to 30 seconds
long.

The gymnast swings around with his body in a piked position. His legs will be out to the sides.

During a routine, a gymnast will use different grips. He will swing both forward and backward. He may swing around holding on with just one arm. It's important to always keep moving

Horizontal Bar

during a routine. Only a gymnast's hands can touch the bar. The last part of the routine is the dismount. The gymnast releases his grip. He may do a twist or somersault. He lands on his feet.

Stretching is an important part of a gymnast's preparation.

Gymnastics is a fun sport. But it also comes with risks. Gymnasts can get hurt if they aren't careful. There are things gymnasts can do to help stay safe.

Every practice should start with a warm-up and stretch. This gets a gymnast's body ready for action. It helps prevent injury. A warm-up might include jogging or doing jumping jacks. This gets the gymnast's heart pumping and blood flowing. It helps warm the muscles. Next comes stretching. Stretches help loosen the muscles. When gymnasts stretch, they usually work on all parts of the body. These include the

neck, shoulders, arms, wrists, back, legs, ankles, and feet. Daily stretching also helps a gymnast become flexible.

There are other ways to stay safe in the gym. Knowing all the rules is important. Gymnasts should be aware of others nearby. They should ask questions if they don't understand something. Gymnasts also learn how to fall properly to help avoid injury. Spotters can help. They stay near a gymnast and help guide them through tricky parts.

Spotters or coaches make sure gymnasts stay safe.
Australian Gymnastics Team
SPiETH

Gyms also have safety equipment. This includes mats. Gyms often have equipment to help people learn new moves, including incline mats and foam pits. Learning how to use the equipment properly can prevent injury. Patience is also important. Gymnastics takes years of practice.

Safety is more than physical. USA Gymnastics has a Safe Sport policy. It helps to make sure that gymnasts feel safe emotionally and mentally. Coaches should never use abusive language. That includes making fun of gymnasts because of their weight or their looks. Coaches shouldn't make

Softening the Blow

Many gymnastics moves are difficult. Gyms often have mats and landing pits filled with foam underneath the apparatus. That lets gymnasts learn and practice without fear of hurting themselves if they fall.

gymnasts feel bad about themselves. Gymnasts should also never be afraid of coaches. If a coach does something to make a gymnast feel scared, the gymnast should talk to a parent or trusted adult.

The right clothing is important for gymnastics. Clothes need to stretch with the body. The fabric also needs to be tight. That lets coaches and judges see the shape a gymnast makes with his or her body during routines.

Girls wear leotards. Leotards fit closely but also stretch. They can have long sleeves or no sleeves. Boys also wear leotards. These are usually sleeveless. Boys wear shorts or tight pants over their leotards.

While practicing or competing, long hair should be tied back. Stray hairs can distract a

gymnast from seeing properly. Gymnasts also shouldn't wear jewelry in the gym. Other pieces of equipment a gymnast might wear are hand guards. Hand guards are used on bars and rings. They help stop blisters and make it easier to swing and circle.

History

People have been doing gymnastics for thousands of years. The ancient Egyptians, Greeks, and Romans all did gymnastics. They practiced in places called gymnasiums. Most schools today have gymnasiums. But the sport was much different in ancient times. There were no uneven bars or still rings. Back then, gymnasts didn't even wear any clothes!

The first modern Olympics were held in 1896. Gymnastics was one of the sports. Only men were included. They competed in horizontal bars, parallel bars, pommel horse, rings, vault, and rope climbing. They also competed in two team events.

Women competed in Olympic gymnastics for the first time in 1928. It looked nothing like women's Olympic gymnastics today. There was only a team competition.

The first World Championship competition was held in 1903. It was just for men. Women were not included until 1934.

When the Soviet Union existed, its gymnasts were among the best in the world. For example, in 1952, the Soviet Union men's team won gold.

Larisa Latynina of the Soviet Union was the star of the 1956 Olympic Games.

The Soviet Union was made up of different republics. The republics included Russia and Ukraine. Year after year, they were difficult to defeat. Japan and East Germany were also good at men's gymnastics for many years.

What Are the Olympics?

The Olympic Games are the most important competition in gymnastics. There are Summer Olympics and Winter Olympics. Gymnastics is a part of the Summer Olympics. The Olympics are held every four years.

Elena Shushunova of the Soviet Union won gold in the all-around competition in 1988.

The Soviet Union women's team often bested its competition. They won eight straight Olympic team gold medals from 1952 to 1980 and then in 1988. Other countries like Hungary and Romania often fought for silver and bronze.

FUN FACT!

Italy's Luigina Giavotti was 11 when she won an Olympic silver medal. She's the youngest medalist in Olympic gymnastics history.

Then came the 1984 Olympics in Los Angeles. The Soviet Union, East Germany, Czechoslovakia, and several other nations did not compete. The United States took the advantage.

The men faced tough competition from China. The US men were up to the challenge. The best score gymnasts could get then was a perfect 10. Mitch Gaylord got a perfect 10 on the rings. Bart Conner got a perfect 10 on the parallel bars.

The US team went to the horizontal bar for the last rotation. Gaylord scored a 9.95. Conner scored a 9.90. Tim Daggett scored a perfect 10. Peter Vidmar scored a 9.95. That was enough for the US team to win team gold for the first time ever.

In the 1984 Olympics, the US men's team won gold.

The US women also did well. The team won the silver medal. Mary Lou Retton became the very first individual all-around gold medalist ever for the United States. Combined, the US men's and women's teams won 16 medals at the 1984 Olympics, including five gold.

Mary Lou Retton of the United States won five medals at the 1984 Olympics.

Life after Gymnastics

Gymnastics careers don't last long. Some gymnasts, like Bart Conner, become coaches and open their own gyms after they retire. Some become judges. Shannon Miller went to law school after she stopped competing. Nastia Liukin became an NBC Olympics analyst. She was a commentator for the Tokyo Games.

The US women have been among the best in the world since the 1990s. They've won an Olympic team medal every year since 1992. From 2011 to 2020, a US woman won every individual Olympic and World Championship gold medal. Simone Biles won six of them. The US women won their sixth straight World Championship title in 2022. It's the longest winning streak in World Championships history.

FUN FACT!

Gabby Douglas became the first Black gymnast to win an Olympic all-around title in 2012. She's also the first US gymnast to win the all-around title and team gold at the same Olympics.

USA Gymnastics Development Program

All gymnasts need a strong foundation. They must master certain skills before safely trying harder ones. USA Gymnastics has a development program. Gymnasts start at Level 1. The program goes through Level 10. Gymnasts build on skills as they advance through the levels.

The women's program has three parts. Developmental is Levels 1 through 3. Gymnasts at this level may or may not compete. Compulsory is Levels 4 and 5. There are more

chances to compete at this level. Optional is Levels 6 through 10. Here the competition gets stronger and harder. The men's program is different. The Essential Elements Program includes Levels 1 through 3. The Age Group Competition Program includes Levels 4 through 10.

Other programs within USA Gymnastics include the Xcel Program, the Future Stars Program, and the HUGS Program.

FUN FACT!

The international governing body for gymnastics is called the International Gymnastics Federation.

High School Gymnastics

Many high school students participate in gymnastics. Most compete through private clubs. Varsity gymnastics is not offered in many high schools in the same way as baseball, softball, basketball, and other sports.

There are several reasons for this. The equipment is expensive. Gymnastics requires a lot of space. Coaches can be hard to find. For boys, state high school teams exist only in Texas, Illinois, Massachusetts, and New York. More states offer girls high school teams, including Pennsylvania and Kansas.

High school gymnast Daniella Jimenez competes in the Texas High School Region III Championship in 2021.

College Gymnastics

Both women and men compete in college gymnastics. The season starts in January. During the season, they usually have one meet each week. Most college gymnasts compete at Level 10 or as elite gymnasts before college. There are some Olympians who go on to compete in college. Some members of the 2021 US women's team competed in the National Collegiate Athletic Association (NCAA) Championships.

US Olympian Grace McCallum later competed for the University of Utah's gymnastics team.

Jordan Chiles competed for the University of California, Los Angeles (UCLA) after participating in the Olympics in 2021.

Only 13 colleges have men's NCAA gymnastics teams. They all compete in one division. There are 81 NCAA women's college teams. They compete in conferences. Conferences hold championships at the end of the season.

The NCAA also has a national championship for men and women. Thirty-six women's teams make the NCAA postseason. It is based on ranking. The top 12 all-around gymnasts and top 16 individual event specialists on each apparatus also qualify for regionals. The top eight teams from regional competitions have a chance to compete for the national championship held every April.

Going Viral

Social media has made some college gymnasts famous. Katelyn Ohashi competed for UCLA. In 2019, she scored a perfect 10 on her floor routine. More than 232 million people have seen the video on YouTube.

Katelyn Ohashi brought more attention to college gymnastics when her 2019 floor routine went viral on social media.

College Meet Format

College women's gymnasts start their routines with a score of 10. Judges take away points for mistakes. A good score would be 9.9. That means the gymnast made only a few small errors. Every gymnast hopes to score a perfect 10.

One type of meet is a dual meet. Two teams compete against one another. In a women's dual meet, the home team starts on the vault and then moves to the uneven bars, balance beam, and floor. Each team picks six gymnasts who compete in each of the four events. Gymnasts perform

Emily White of Arizona State performs a floor exercise in 2022.

The University of Oklahoma's Yul Moldauer competes on the pommel horse.

two routines per event. The top five scores count toward the team combined score.

Men's college gymnastics is different. The men use the same scoring as international gymnastics. Five gymnasts from each school compete in each event. All five scores count.

Top Women's College Teams

The University of Utah won the first women's NCAA gymnastics title in 1982. Since then, only seven different schools have won the championship. The University of Georgia has won the most. Georgia has won the title ten times. Utah has won nine. Thousands of fans come to Utah's meets. Sometimes they have more fans than pro basketball and hockey teams.

The University of Oklahoma won the NCAA championship in 2022. It was the school's fifth title in eight years. Ragan Smith, an Olympic alternate in 2016, clinched the title with her balance beam routine. Other schools that have won titles in previous years include UCLA, the University of Alabama, the University of Florida, and the University of Michigan.

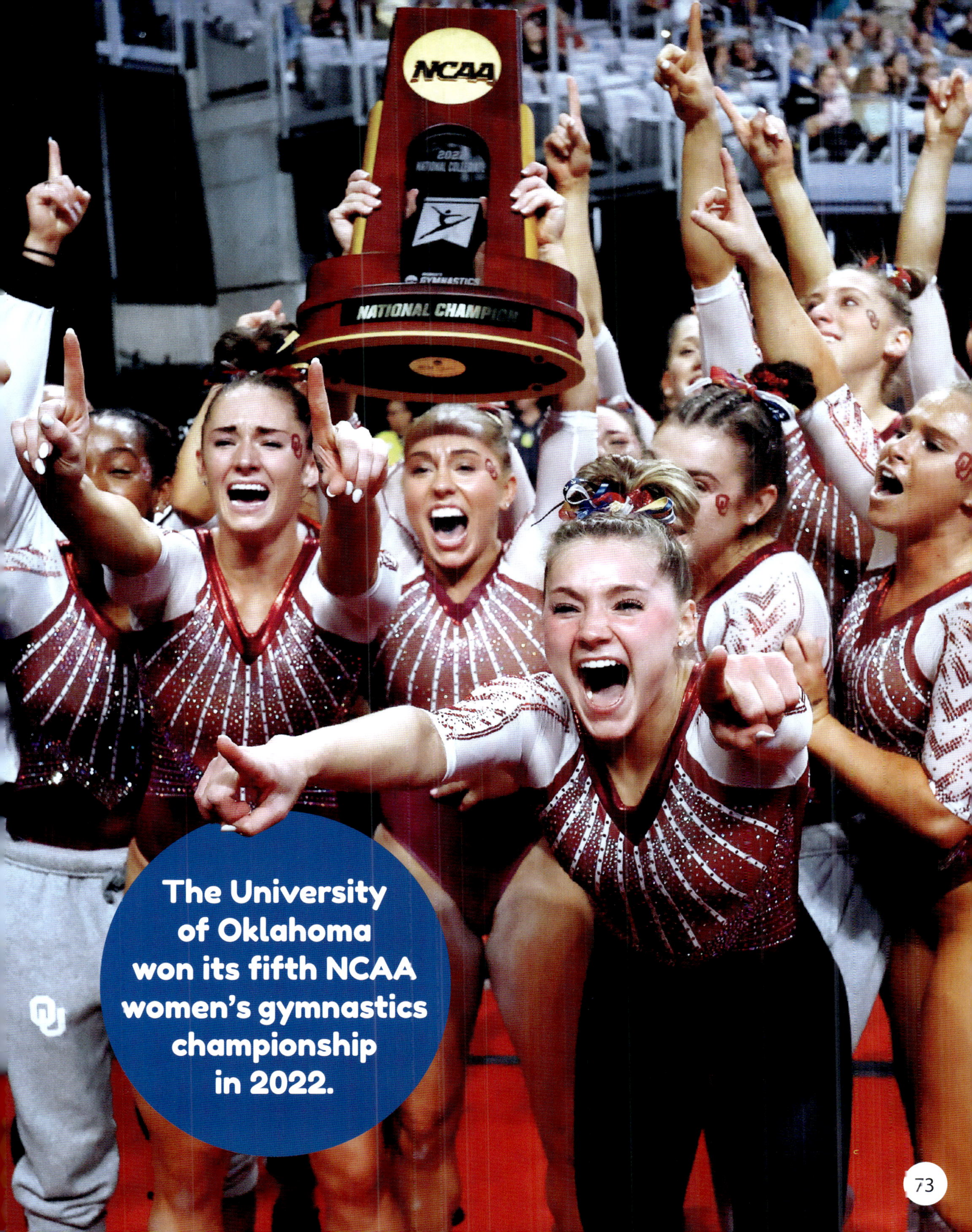

NCAA
NATIONAL CHAMPION
The University of Oklahoma won its fifth NCAA women's gymnastics championship in 2022.

Top Men's College Teams

The University of Oklahoma and Penn State have each won 12 NCAA team titles. No other school has won more. Two-time Olympic gold medalist Bart Conner went to Oklahoma. So did USA Gymnastics Hall of Famer and Olympic silver medalist Jonathan Horton.

Stanford won its third NCAA title in a row in 2022. Oklahoma was the runner-up all three years. Before that,

Jonathan Horton celebrates after sticking the landing on the still rings in 2010.

Oklahoma won four years in a row. Illinois has ten NCAA titles. Nebraska and Stanford each have eight.

Elite Gymnastics

Many young girls and boys take gymnastics lessons. Very few will become elite gymnasts. Becoming an elite gymnast is the first step toward earning a spot on the national team. National team athletes represent the United States at international meets including the Olympics. There are both junior elites and senior elites.

Gymnasts need to practice regularly to make the national team.

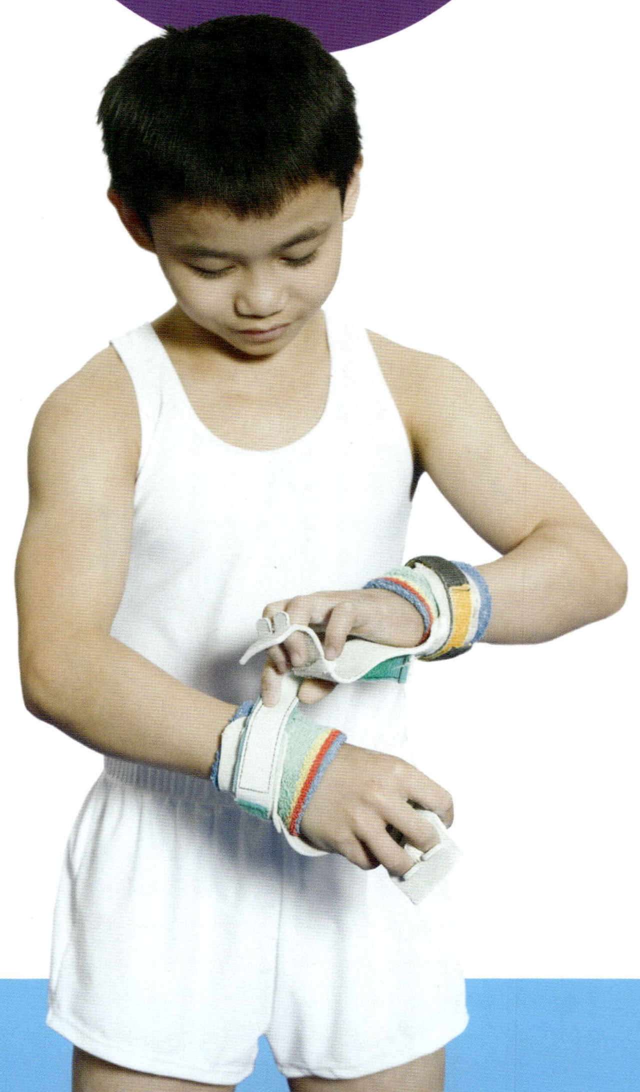

Vitaly Scherbo of Belarus holds the record for most Olympic gold medals at one Games. He won six out of eight gymnastics events in 1992.

Most elite gymnasts start taking classes at a young age.

A Day in the Life of an Elite Gymnast

Being an elite gymnast takes commitment. Six-time Olympic medalist Aly Raisman trained for 35 hours every week preparing for the 2016 Olympic Games in Rio de Janeiro, Brazil. She woke up at 7 a.m. and practiced for about three hours. Then she ate lunch. Raisman went back to the gym and practiced for four hours. She didn't eat dinner until 9:40 p.m. She went to bed at 10:15 p.m.

Raisman needed to eat healthy to get energy.

Olympian Aly Raisman worked with a nutritionist to maintain a healthy diet while training.

A strict
training routine
helped MyKayla
Skinner return to elite
gymnastics and make
the Olympics after
competing in
college.

Foods with high protein, such as salmon, are an important part of an elite gymnast's diet.

Her typical lunch included grilled chicken and vegetables. For dinner, she usually ate salmon and vegetables.

Simone Biles won four gold medals at the 2016 Olympics in Rio. She also won one bronze medal. Biles trained seven hours a day, six days a week to get ready for the Tokyo Olympics.

MyKayla Skinner is another Olympian. Her routine included training at different stations in a gym. The exercises helped make her strong. She sometimes practiced one move on the uneven bars over and over.

Everyone's day may be slightly different. What each routine has in common is lots of practice and hard work. Eating healthy meals and getting enough rest are also important pieces of an elite gymnast's day.

Elite Competitions

There aren't many major elite gymnastics meets in a year. Each one is very important. Some help athletes to qualify for the national team or for bigger meets. Here are some of the biggest meets:

Winter Cup

This is usually the first big men's competition of every year. It is held in February.

US Classic

This is an annual summer meet before nationals. It used to be only for women. Men were invited in 2022. Simone Biles won five times. Aly Raisman won three. It is the final qualifier for the national championships.

Yul Moldauer competes on the pommel horse at the 2021 Winter Cup.

US Championships

The national champions in US gymnastics are named at this late-summer meet. Champs are crowned in the all-around and for each apparatus. In addition, results from this meet

Brody Malone gets ready to compete on the still rings in the 2021 US Championships.

help determine the teams for the Olympics and World Championships.

Gymnastics World Cups

This is an international series of competitions. It includes the Individual All-Around World Cup Series, the Individual Apparatus World Cup Series, and the World Challenge Cup Series.

Nina Derwael of Belgium performs on the balance beam in the 2021 FIG World Challenge Cup.

Olympic Team Trials

The Trials are held every summer before the Olympics. This is the last meet before the Games. It helps determine who will compete in the Olympics.

Gabby Douglas gets emotional after being named to the 2012 US Olympic team.

World Championships

The World Championships for men and women take place every year except Olympic years. The 2022 World Championships took place in Liverpool, England.

Olympic and World Championship Meet Format

Major gymnastics championships, including the Olympic Games, begin with a qualifying round. The teams and gymnasts with the best scores in qualifying then advance to the finals. Men and women each have a team and individual all-around final. Men also have individual finals for each of the six apparatuses. Women have four individual apparatus finals.

In team qualifying, four gymnasts from a country compete on each apparatus. The top three scores on each apparatus are added together.

Gymnasts must perform well in the qualifying round at the Olympics in order to advance to an event final.

This creates a team score. Eight countries qualify for the team final. There, three gymnasts per country compete in each event. All three scores are counted.

Twenty-four gymnasts qualify for the individual all-around finals. They perform a routine on each apparatus. Those scores are then combined to create an all-around score. Eight gymnasts qualify for each individual event final. They perform a routine once in the final.

For individual finals, only two gymnasts per country can advance. That means if one country has the top three gymnasts in qualifying for an event, only the first two can compete in finals.

Many
athletes
are proud to
represent their
countries in the
Olympics.

Sawao Kato, Japan

Japan had one of the best men's gymnastics teams in the world in the 1960s and '70s. Sawao Kato was its star. He faced a tough competition against the Soviet Union at the 1968 Olympics. However, he won three gold medals and one bronze medal.

Sawao Kato, *center*, won the gold medal in the men's all-around event in the 1972 Olympics.

Four years later, he repeated as Olympic all-around champion. Japan won its fourth team gold medal. In the event finals, Kato won gold on the parallel bars, silver on vault, and bronze on horizontal bar.

Kato competed for the last time at the Olympics in 1976. He repeated as parallel bars champion. Kato still holds the record for most Olympic gold medals by a men's gymnast, with eight.

Nikolai Andrianov, Soviet Union

The Soviet Union was a powerhouse in men's gymnastics for many years. Nikolai Andrianov was one of the reasons. He had powerful moves and difficult skills. If everyone else was doing a double flip dismount, he'd do a triple.

Andrianov's best events were floor exercise and rings, but he could do anything. He won his first three Olympic medals in 1972 when he was 19. One was gold in floor exercise. One was silver in the team competition. The third was bronze in vault. That was only the beginning.

His best year was 1976. He won seven medals and was champion in the all-around, floor exercise, rings, and vault. He won five more medals in 1980. His 15 medals were a men's Olympic record for many years.

Nikolai Andrianov was added to the International Gymnastics Hall of Fame in 2001.

Larisa Latynina, Soviet Union

Larisa Latynina last competed at the Olympics in 1964. Yet her 18 Olympic medals remained a record among all athletes for nearly 50 years. Through 2023, no woman had won more.

Latynina was from the Soviet Union. She took ballet classes as a young girl. That helped her become an elegant and creative gymnast. Her favorite event was the floor exercise because she could express herself.

Latynina made her Olympic debut in 1956 when she was 21 years old. She won gold in the all-around, vault, and floor exercise. She also helped the Soviet Union win team gold. She knew she wanted more. In the 1960 Olympics, Latynina won six medals. She won another six in 1964. Nine of Latynina's medals were gold. She was the floor exercise champion in all three Olympics.

Larisa
Latynina has
18 Olympic medals,
which is the second
most of any athlete
in Olympic
history.

Olga Korbut, Soviet Union

Olga Korbut was one of the first superstars of gymnastics. She competed in the 1970s for the Soviet Union. Korbut wasn't afraid to try new things. Her fearlessness would change women's gymnastics.

Korbut was 17 years old when she made her Olympic debut in 1972. Her first event was the balance beam. Korbut did a backflip. No one had ever done that in international competition at the time. Korbut won the gold medal. She also won gold on floor and in the team competition.

Olga Korbut was a creative and daring gymnast.

Then she stunned the world again on the uneven bars. She stood on the high bar. Then she did a backflip. She caught the high bar and then released and flipped around the low bar. As she came around, she reached back and caught the high bar again. No one could believe what they saw. The move was called the Korbut Flip.

Nadia Comaneci, Romania

Four years after Olga Korbut's flip came Nadia Comaneci from Romania. She was just 14 when she arrived in Montreal for the 1976 Olympic Games. She was about to make history.

Gymnastics was scored on a scale from 1 to 10. No one had ever scored a 10, though. Then Comaneci took her turn on the uneven

Nadia Comaneci won three gold medals at the 1976 Montreal Olympics.

Comaneci does her routine on the balance beam during the 1976 Olympics.

bars, and she did it better than anyone. The scoreboard showed a 1.00. It wasn't even set up to display her perfect score. She'd done the impossible.

Comaneci scored six more perfect 10s during those Olympics. She won gold in the all-around, balance beam, and uneven bars. She also won a team silver medal and bronze on floor exercise. Her picture was on magazine covers everywhere.

Mary Lou Retton, United States

For many years, athletes from the Soviet Union were the best at women's gymnastics. In 1984, the United States hosted the Olympics in Los Angeles. The Soviet Union did not come. A 16-year-old from West Virginia named Mary Lou Retton took her turn to shine and became a star.

Retton led the all-around competition going into the last rotation. She was only 0.15 points ahead of the second-place athlete. Retton's last event was the vault. She needed a perfect 10. Retton twisted through the air and stuck the landing. Her routine scored a perfect 10!

Retton became the first American woman to win gold in the all-around. She also won three more medals. The women's team won silver. No one else won more than five medals at the 1984 Summer Olympics.

Retton was the first woman to have her photo on a Wheaties box. *Sports Illustrated* named her Sportswoman of the Year. Retton was a superstar.

Bart Conner, United States

No American man has accomplished more in gymnastics than Bart Conner. Conner was ten when he started gymnastics at the YMCA. He was 14 when he won the junior national championship. Then he became the youngest US all-around champion at 17. He had just finished high school and was the youngest member of the men's 1976 Olympic gymnastics team.

Conner made history again in 1979. He won the pommel horse at the World Cup and became a world champion in the

Bart Conner led the 1984 US men's team to the Olympic title.

parallel bars. No US gymnast had ever won gold medals at those meets.

In 1984, the United States hosted the Summer Olympics. Conner was recovering from an injury, but he was ready. His perfect 10 on the parallel bars helped the team win its first gold medal in Olympic history. He also won gold on the parallel bars.

Shannon Miller, United States

Before there was Simone Biles, there was Shannon Miller. She was the most decorated US gymnast for many years. Miller was an excellent all-around gymnast. She made her Olympic debut in 1992 when she was 15. Although she didn't win gold, Miller won five medals. That was more than any other US athlete at the 1992 Olympics.

Miller returned to the 1996 Olympics in Atlanta. She helped lead the United States to its first team gold medal. Then Miller won a second gold medal on the balance beam. At the time, her seven Olympic medals and nine World Championship medals were the most ever won by an American gymnast. Miller was inducted into the US Olympic and Paralympic Hall of Fame twice. Once was on her own, and once was with the 1996 team.

Shannon Miller was the first US gymnast to win two back-to-back world all-around titles.

The Magnificent Seven, United States

All eyes were on the US women during the team competition at the Atlanta Olympics in 1996. Their nickname was the Magnificent Seven. They were Shannon Miller, Dominique Dawes,

The Magnificent Seven became the first US women's gymnastics team to win an Olympic gold medal.

Dominique Moceanu, Kerri Strug, Amy Chow, Jaycie Phelps, and team captain Amanda Borden. Everyone knew they were good.

The US team held a slim lead over Russia going into the last rotation. They were on the vault. Moceanu was the youngest member of the team. She was 14. She had the chance to clinch the gold medal. But she slipped and fell on both her vaults. It was all up to Strug.

Though Strug was the team's best vaulter, she fell on the first attempt. She also hurt her ankle. She limped back to try again. Strug ran toward the vault and launched into the air. She landed a one-and-a-half twisting Yurchenko. Right away she picked up her left leg. She hopped on her right. She'd hurt her left ankle. But the score came up at 9.712. She had done it! The US women won their first Olympic gold medal.

Paul Hamm, United States

Paul Hamm grew up in a small town in Wisconsin. As a kid he swung from the rafters in his family's barn. He practiced on a pommel horse made from a maple tree. And eventually he became the best gymnast in the world.

Paul Hamm poses during his floor exercise in the 2004 Olympic Team Trials.

Hamm celebrates his gold medal win at the 2004 Olympics.

In 2003, Hamm was in competition for the all-around title at the World Championships. His last event was the horizontal bar. He needed a great score to beat Chinese gymnast Yang Wei.

Hamm's routine included four straight release moves. He scored a 9.975 and won the all-around gold medal. He was the first American man to become an all-around world champion.

One year later, Hamm went to the Olympics in Athens, Greece. He helped the US team win the silver medal. It was their first team medal in 20 years. Next up was the all-around. Hamm scored 9.837. He won gold by 0.049 points. It was the closest finish ever in the Olympic men's all-around. Hamm was the first US man to win the Olympic all-around title.

After receiving his horizontal bar score at the Athens Olympics, Hamm and his coach celebrate.

Nastia Liukin, United States

Nastia Liukin has gymnastics in her blood. Her father, Valeri, was a two-time Olympic gold medalist in 1988. Her mother, Anna Kotchneva, won a World Championship in rhythmic gymnastics. Liukin was known for being a graceful gymnast. She had a very elegant style. Her best events were uneven bars and the balance beam.

In 2008, Liukin made her Olympic debut. Many people thought her teammate Shawn Johnson would win the all-around gold.

Nastia Liukin won five medals at the 2008 Olympics in Beijing, China.

Liukin competes at the 2008 Pacific Rim Gymnastics Championships.

Johnson had won the title at both the national championships and the Olympic Trials. Johnson was also the reigning world champion. Liukin and Johnson were each other's toughest competition.

It all came down to the floor exercise. Liukin ended up winning gold by sixth-tenths of a point. She also won a total of five medals that year. She matched the US record shared by Mary Lou Retton and Shannon Miller for most medals in one Olympics.

Dancing with the Gymnasts

Many Olympic gymnasts have appeared on the television show *Dancing with the Stars*, including Simone Biles, Aly Raisman, and Mary Lou Retton. Shawn Johnson and Laurie Hernandez won the Mirrorball Trophy for their performances. This trophy is given to the winning couple.

Liukin placed fourth on season 20 of *Dancing with the Stars.*

Kohei Uchimura, Japan

It's extremely hard to win a world or Olympic title. For eight years in a row, Japan's Kohei Uchimura was undefeated. He was good at everything. People loved watching his power and grace. Many call him one of the greatest male gymnasts of all time.

Uchimura made his Olympic debut in 2008. He won silver in the all-around. It was Japan's first medal in the event since Sawao Kato won gold in 1972. One year later, Uchimura won his first all-around title at the World Championships.

When he went to the next Olympics in 2012, Uchimura was a three-time defending world champion. He won again in London, and more titles followed. He won three more World Championships.

Then at the 2016 Olympics in Rio, Uchimura cemented his legacy with a second Olympic

all-around gold medal. It took a daring horizontal bar routine to win. Uchimura also helped Japan win the team gold. Uchimura was the first man since Kato to win back-to-back Olympic titles.

The Final Five, United States

The US team of Simone Biles, Aly Raisman, Laurie Hernandez, Gabby Douglas, and Madison Kocian were favorites at the 2016 Olympics. The US women had won every international team competition since 2011. That meant there was a lot of pressure. But they were up to the task.

They won the team title by a large margin. The Olympic format was switching to four gymnasts per country after the 2016 Rio Olympics. So the squad called themselves "the Final Five."

After winning the team title, Biles and Raisman finished first and second in the all-around. The US women won nine medals that year. No US team had ever won that many.

Aly Raisman and Simone Biles pose with their Olympic medals.

Simone Biles, United States

There's never been a gymnast like Simone Biles. She does things no one else can do. Biles made her Olympic debut in Rio in 2016. She was 19 and already a three-time world all-around champion. Biles put on a show. Her team won the gold medal, and Biles won the all-around title. She performed a skill on the floor that had never been done. It was named the Biles.

Simone Biles earned her reputation as the most dominant athlete in the sport's history.

Name That Skill

Simone Biles has four skills named after her. In order to have a skill named after her, a woman has to be the first one to perform the skill successfully at either the World Championships or Olympics. A man can perform his skill at a World Cup, World Challenge, the World Championships, or the Olympics.

Simone Biles won five gold medals at the 2019 World Championships.

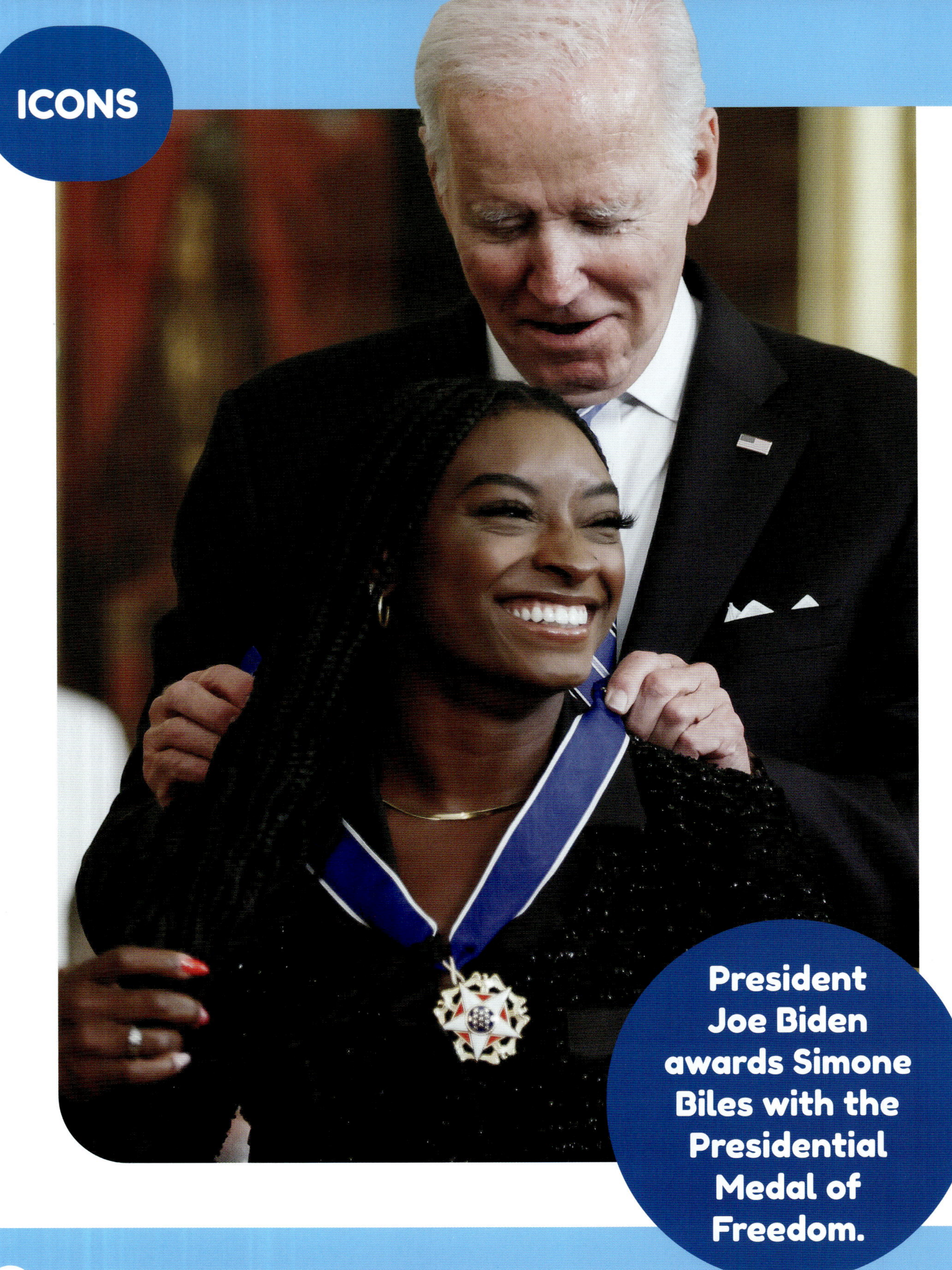

President Joe Biden awards Simone Biles with the Presidential Medal of Freedom.

Biles returned to the next Olympics, which were held in 2021 in Tokyo. She started the team competition. But something didn't feel right. She lost track of where her body was in the air.

She ended up withdrawing from the team and all-around competitions. Her mental health was more important than winning medals. It was a brave decision. She returned for the balance beam final and won bronze. She also won team silver. Biles has won 32 Olympic and World Championship medals.

Biles in the Books

Simone Biles owns a number of World Championship records. No one has won more medals than her 25 or more gold medals than her 19. She's also the first woman to win five all-around titles, five floor exercise titles, and three balance beam titles.

GLOSSARY

all-around
An individual competition in which the gymnast competes on every piece of apparatus.

apparatus
A piece of equipment used in gymnastics.

balance
The ability to stay still and controlled.

dismount
The last move of a routine when a gymnast leaves the apparatus and returns to the floor.

endurance
The ability to stay strong when performing difficult athletic activities over time, such as during a routine.

execution
How well a gymnast performs a skill or routine.

handspring
Flipping from the feet to the hands, pushing off and flipping back to the feet.

rotations
Forward or backward movements in a circle.

salto
A flip or a somersault.

specialist
Someone who focuses most on one piece of apparatus.

springboard
A piece of equipment that the gymnast jumps on to bounce up to a vault table, balance beam, or other apparatus.

stick the landing
When a gymnast dismounts and lands on the floor without any hops or steps.

More Books to Read

Abdo, Kenny. *History of Gymnastics*. Abdo, 2020.

Flynn, Sarah Wassner. *Gymnastics*. National Geographic Kids, 2020.

Walduck, Vincent. *My Book of Gymnastics*. DK Publishing, 2020.

Online Resources

To learn more about gymnastics, please visit **abdobooklinks.com** or scan this QR code. These links are routinely monitored and updated to provide the most current information available.

INDEX

Cover Photos: Sergey Golotvin/Shutterstock Images, front (left); Jamie Squire/Getty Images Sport/Getty Images, front (middle); Shutterstock Images, front (right); Alex Bogatyrev/Shutterstock Images, front (background); Michael C. Gray/Shutterstock Images, back

Interior Photos: Shutterstock Images, 1, 10, 12–13, 16, 19, 23, 34, 37, 38, 43, 44, 45, 46, 62; Real Sports Photos/Shutterstock Images, 3, 7, 24, 50, 63; Patrick Smith/Getty Images Sport/Getty Images, 4–5; Svitlana Bezuhlova/Shutterstock Images, 6; Peter Byrne/PA Images/Getty Images, 8; David Madison/Getty Images Sport/Getty Images, 9, 105, 108; Stew Milne/Getty Images Sport/Getty Images, 11; Alex Bogatyrev/Shutterstock Images, 14, 28, 47; Michael C. Gray/Shutterstock Images, 15 (top left), 15 (top right); Amri Photo/iStockphoto, 15 (bottom); Jiang Dao Hua/Shutterstock Images, 17; Fabrice Coffrini/AFP/Getty Images, 20; Paolo Bona/Shutterstock Images, 21; Ian MacNicol/Getty Images Sport/Getty Images, 22; Laurence Griffiths/Getty Images Sport/Getty Images, 25, 32, 36, 88–89; Tim Clayton/Corbis Sport/Getty Images, 26, 87; Maja Hitij/Getty Images Sport/Getty Images, 27, 79; Tony Ding/Icon SMI/Corbis/Icon Sportswire/Getty Images, 29; iStockphoto, 31 (top), 31 (bottom), 76, 77, 80; Wang Xianmin/CHINASPORTS/VCG/Getty Images, 33; Lluis Gene/AFP/Getty Images, 35 (left); Nick Laham/Getty Images Sport/Getty Images, 35 (right); Naomi Baker/Getty Images Sport/Getty Images, 41, 42; Koki Nagahama/Getty Images Sport/Getty Images, 49; Vitalii Smulskyi/Shutterstock Images, 51 (left); Antonio Diaz/Shutterstock Images, 51 (right); Milos Bicanski/Getty Images Sport/Getty Images, 52; Bob Thomas/Popperfoto/Getty Images, 53; George Rinhart/Corbis Historical/Getty Images, 54; AFP/Getty Images, 55; Tony Duffy/Getty Images Sport/Getty Images, 56, 104; Sadayuki Mikami/AP Images, 57; Wally McNamee/Corbis Historical/Getty Images, 58–59, 100; Steve Ross/Hulton Archive/Archive Photos/Getty Images, 60; Streeter Lecka/Getty Images Sport/Getty Images, 61; Jacob Ford/Odessa American/AP Images, 64–65; C. Morgan Engel/NCAA Photos/Getty Images, 66, 73; Katharine Lotze/Getty Images Sport/Getty Images, 67, 69; Zac BonDurant/Icon Sportswire/Getty Images, 70; Steve Woltmann/NCAA Photos/Getty Images, 71; Michael Tureski/Icon SMI/Icon Sport Media/Icon Sportswire/Getty Images, 74; Isaiah Vazquez/NCAA Photos/Getty Images, 75; Michael Regan/Getty Images Sport/Getty Images, 78; Milla F./Shutterstock Images, 81; Jamie Squire/Getty Images Sport/Getty Images, 83, 84; Davor Javorovic/Pixsell/MB Media/Getty Images Sport/Getty Images, 85; Ezra Shaw/Getty Images Sport/Getty Images, 86, 122; Alex Livesey/Getty Images Sport/Getty Images, 90–91, 119, 121; AP Images, 92, 93, 99;Universal/Corbis/VCG/Sygma/Getty Images, 95; The Asahi Shimbun/Getty Images, 97; Focus on Sport/Getty Images Sport/Getty Images, 98, 103; Don Morley/Hulton Archive/Getty Images, 101; Simon Bruty/Allsport/Hulton Archive/Getty Images, 107; Stephen Dunn/Getty Images Sport/Getty Images, 110; Donald Miralle/Getty Images Sport/Getty Images, 111; Adam Pretty/Getty Images Sport/Getty Images, 113; Scott Halleran/Getty Images for VISA/Getty Images Sport/Getty Images, 114; Greg Trott/Getty Images Sport/Getty Images, 115; Allen Berezovsky/Getty Images Entertainment/Getty Images, 117; Ben Stansall/AFP/Getty Images, 120; Thomas Kienzle/AFP/Getty Images, 123; Alex Wong/Getty Images News/Getty Images, 124